Nati

Terry Pratchett is one of the most popular authors writing today.
He is the acclaimed creator of the Discworld series, the first title
of which, *The Colour of Magic*, was published in 1983: the latest,
number 37, is *Unseen Academicals*. His first Discworld novel for
children, *The Amazing Maurice and his Educated Rodents*, was
awarded the 2001 Carnegie Medal. Worldwide sales of his books
are now 65 million, and they have been published in 37 languages.
Terry Pratchett was knighted for services to literature in 2009.
Visit www.terrypratchett.co.uk for news and information,
to join the forum and to register for updates.

Mark Ravenhill's first full-length play, *Shopping and Fucking*,
opened at the Royal Court Theatre Upstairs in September 1996.
His other works include *Faust is Dead* (ATC, UK tour, 1997);
Sleeping Around, a joint venture with three other writers (Salisbury
Playhouse, 1998); *Handbag* (Lyric Hammersmith Studio, 1998);
Some Explicit Polaroids (Theatre Royal, Bury St Edmunds, 1999);
Mother Clap's Molly House (National Theatre, 2001); *Totally Over
You* (National Theatre, 2003); *Product* (Traverse Theatre, Edinburgh,
2005); *The Cut* (Donmar Warehouse, London, 2006); *Citizenship*
(National Theatre, 2006); *pool (no water)* (Lyric Hammersmith,
2006); *Shoot/Get Treasure/Repeat* (Edinburgh Festival, 2007 –
Fringe First and a Spirit of the Fringe Award); *Over There* (Royal
Court/Schaubühne, Berlin, 2009); and *A Life in Three Acts*,
co-written with Bette Bourne (Traverse Theatre, Edinburgh/
Konninklijke Schouwburg, The Hague/Soho Theatre, London,
2009 – Fringe First and the Herald Archangel Award).

THE DISCWORLD NOVELS

The Discworld® series: have you read them all?

OTHER BOOKS ABOUT DISCWORLD

THE ART OF DISCWORLD
(with Paul Kidby)
THE WIT AND WISDOM OF DISCWORLD
(compiled by Stephen Briggs)
THE FOLKLORE OF DISCWORLD
(with Jacqueline Simpson)

DISCWORLD MAPS

THE STREETS OF ANKH-MORPORK
(with Stephen Briggs)
THE DISCWORLD MAPP
(with Stephen Briggs)
A TOURIST GUIDE TO LANCRE –
A DISCWORLD MAPP
(with Stephen Briggs, illustrated by Paul Kidby)
DEATH'S DOMAIN
(with Paul Kidby)

A complete list of other books based on the Discworld series
– illustrated screenplays, graphic novels, comics and plays –
can be found on www.terrypratchett.co.uk

NON-DISCWORLD BOOKS

THE DARK SIDE OF THE SUN
STRATA
THE UNADULTERATED CAT
(illustrated by Gray Jolliffe)
GOOD OMENS
(with Neil Gaiman)

Nation

a play adapted for the stage by
MARK RAVENHILL

from the novel by
TERRY PRATCHETT

CORGI BOOKS

TRANSWORLD PUBLISHERS
61–63 Uxbridge Road, London W5 5SA
A Random House Group Company
www.rbooks.co.uk

NATION: THE PLAY
A Corgi Book 9780552162159

First publication in Great Britain
Corgi edition published 2009

Addresses for Random House Group Ltd companies
outside the UK can be found at: www.randomhouse.co.uk

The Random House Group Ltd Reg. No. 954009

The Random House Group Limited supports The Forest Stewardship
Council (FSC), the leading international forest certification organisation.
All our titles that are printed on Greenpeace approved FSC certified paper
carry the FSC logo. Our paper procurement policy can be found at
www.rbooks.co.uk/environment

Designed and typeset in Sabon by Country Setting,
Kingsdown, Kent CT14 8ES

Printed in the UK by CPI Cox & Wyman, Reading RGI 8EX

2 4 6 8 10 9 7 5 3 1

FIRST PERFORMANCE

11 November 2009, in the Olivier auditorium
of the National Theatre, London

MAU	Gary Carr
DAPHNE	Emily Taaffe
MILTON, A PARROT	Jason Thorpe
CAPTAIN ROBERTS	David Sterne
POLEGRAVE	Al Nedjari
FOXLIP	Michael Mears
COX	Paul Chahidi
MAU'S FATHER	Bhasker Patel
GRANDMOTHER	Gaye Brown
ATABA	Ewart James Walters
MILO	David Ajala
PILU	Craig Stein
CAHLE	Sirine Saba
MARISGALA	Lorna Gayle
DAPHNE'S FATHER	Nicholas Rowe
THE JUDY	Itxaso Moreno

Gentlemen of Last Resort
Elaine Claxton, Howard Gossington, Robert Hastie,
Nick Malinowski, David Sterne

Islanders and Raiders
Elaine Claxton, Adrian Decosta, Mike Denman,
Nancy Wei George, Howard Gossington, Tony Hasnath,
Robert Hastie, Amy Loughton, Michelle Lukes,
Nick Malinowski, Gurpreet Singh, David Sterne

All other parts played by members of the company

Director	Melly Still
Set Designers	Melly Still with Mark Friend
Costume Designer	Dinah Collin

Puppets and Puppetry	Yvonne Stone
Lighting Designer	Paul Anderson
Projection Designers	Jon Driscoll and
	Gemma Carrington
Composer	Adrian Sutton
Sound Designer	Paul Arditti
Music Director	Martin Lowe
Fight Director	Paul Benzing
Choreography	The Company

*This text went to press before the first performance,
so will not include any changes made
in the final weeks of rehearsal.*

CHARACTERS

MAU
DAPHNE
MILTON, A PARROT
CAPTAIN ROBERTS
FOXLIP
POLEGRAVE
COX
MAU'S FATHER
LOCAHA
DAPHNE'S GRANDMOTHER
CHIEF RAIDER
ATABA
MILO
PILU
CAHLE
TWINKLE
MARISGALA
DAPHNE'S FATHER
COX'S SON
I-TO
MAN
BOY
GIRL
FIVE GENTLEMEN OF THE LAST RESORT

SAILORS
ISLANDERS
GRANDFATHERS
RAIDERS
SOLDIERS

GRANDFATHER BIRDS
A SOW WITH PIGLETS
SHARKS
DOLPHINS

Nation

Act One

PROLOGUE

Mau raises an axe.

MAU   Mah!

               *Mau brings the axe down hard until
               it is stuck in a tree.*

               *An explosion of birds in all directions
               calling out in warning and alarm.*

               Huge rolling thunder.

               Mau runs.

ONE

*Thunder. Great flashes of lightning. A huge storm at
sea. The deck of the* Sweet Judy. *Sailors rush around,
desperate to save the ship.*

SAILORS   We're taking in water. She's breaking
               up. We're going down. Abandon
               ship!

               *Daphne, aged twelve and in Victorian
               clothing, appears from below, runs
               along the deck with Milton, the ship's
               parrot.*

DAPHNE   What's happening?

MILTON   Abandon ship!

           Captain Roberts appears above.

ROBERTS   Tie me fast.

           Several soldiers tie Roberts to the wheel. He sings an evangelical hymn.

DAPHNE   Captain Roberts!

MILTON   Captain Roberts.

DAPHNE   What are your instructions?

ROBERTS   The light is so bright. He's calling me to march amongst the chosen ones. Oh rapture! Oh everlasting light!

           Polegrave approaches.

POLEGRAVE He's no use. In heaven already.

DAPHNE   Put me on a lifeboat.

POLEGRAVE Every man for himself.

           Foxlip approaches.

FOXLIP   Only one boat left. Come on.

DAPHNE   Foxlip, take me with you.

POLEGRAVE No bloody way. Bad luck. No women. No parrot.

DAPHNE   My father is 139th in line to the throne—

POLEGRAVE	Off we go. Come hell and high water.
DAPHNE	Won't one of you help me? I—
FOXLIP	Polegrave!

They've gone.

Daphne bangs on a trapdoor.

DAPHNE	Cox? Cox! Help me. The ship's breaking up.

Daphne goes below deck to Cox.

COX	Let a fellow sleep, can't you?
DAPHNE	Cox – you've been drinking. Grandmother would not approve—
COX	Damn your grandmother and damn you, Miss Ermintrude.
DAPHNE	That is hardly the way for a butler to—
COX	I'm no butler now. I'm a dead man. You're a dead man. We're all dead men.
MILTON	In heaven already.
COX	We're all going to be taken just like my boy was taken. Let it take yer.
DAPHNE	My father is waiting for me in Port Mercia.
MILTON	Oh rapture! Oh everlasting light!

COX	Shut your noise, parrot. Whole voyage in me head.
MILTON	Every man for himself.
COX	Silence. You bugger.

Cox fires at the parrot, who falls.

DAPHNE	Milton!
SAILOR	Great big wave. Bigger than the world. Look!
COX	The biggest wave there ever was. Nothing for ever more.
MILTON	I can see the light.
COX	Die! Die! Die!

Daphne finds a flare, which she fires. The lightning and thunder grow even louder. Cox fires wildly as Milton swears, Daphne cries help and signals, Roberts sings wildly. Cox fires a cannon. A giant wave consumes them all.

A great swirling mass of bodies, prominent among them Daphne and Mau, wood, fish and water. The God Anchors swirl in the tumult. The tree with the axe tumbles towards Mau. He grabs hold of it for a moment but is then pulled away.

TWO

Silence. Mau is unconscious on the beach.

FATHER   (*off*) Mau, Mau!

Enter Mau's Father.

FATHER   Come, Mau! Wake up.

MAU   Father. What happened?

FATHER   You're back from the small island. Did you put the axe in the tree as I told you? Your mother and the other women are excited. Soon you will have your sunset tattoo. You will be a man as I am.

MAU   There was—

FATHER   Yes?

MAU   There was a great big wave – the biggest – first the sea was bubbling and then it was shaking and then it was . . . so hot the fish burnt.

FATHER   Mau. One of your dreams. Here come the Nation.

Enter the Nation, all wearing masks, singing and dancing. Father puts his mask on.

A masked Islander representing
Mau's Man-Soul comes forward.

NATION

Imo made the sea
Imo made the fish
Imo made the dolphins
Imo used a dolphin's soul
And Imo made the people.

We're born in water
Don't kill dolphins
Look to the stars.

Imo made too many
Imo took the night
Imo made Locaha
Locaha made the people die
And turned them into dolphins.

We're born in water
Don't kill dolphins
Look to the stars.

Imo lives up above us
Imo made the stars
Imo made a perfect world
Imo made the gods who watch
Over Imo's people.

We're born in water
Don't kill dolphins
Look to the stars.

MAN

I am your man-soul. Are you ready
for me?

MAU	I am ready for you.
MAN	First: what must a man do?
MAU	A man must look after other men. A man must guard the Nation. A man must listen to the Ancestors. A man must protect the God Anchors.
MAN	You have no soul. Around your neck hangs the blue crab, the sign that you are between boy-soul and man-soul. Give me the crab so that you can become a man.
MAU	I . . .

Pause.

MAN	Give me the crab so that you can become a man.

Pause.

FATHER	Mau. You must.
MAU	I can't do it.
FATHER	But this is the ceremony.
MAU	But still I—
FATHER	Son. Are you afraid to become a man?
MAU	No. But.
FATHER	Then give the blue crab shell.

MAN   Give me the crab shell so that—

MAU   I won't do it. There was a wave. That was no dream. There is some—

FATHER   You will anger the ancestors.

MAU   There's a trick here.

Mau rips the mask off the face of the Man-Soul to reveal a contorted face below. The man screams and falls to the floor in contorted death.

FATHER   Have you lost your mind?

MAU   How many of you?

Mau rips off two more masks. The same thing happens.

FATHER   I had a manhood ceremony. Your grandfather. Back through time. Why must you destroy this, Mau?

MAU   Something is wrong here. Take off your masks. Show me who you are.

The rest take off their masks. They scream and die.

FATHER   Oh, my son. The Nation is dead. Your mother. Your sister. Look, here she is. Your old friend Nawi. Take a look. All of them stuffed full with water when the great wave came until there was no more life in them. Oh Mau, what shall we do?

MAU   Are they all dead?

FATHER   All. Where once there was a Nation
               now there are only corpses. Come
               here and let me hold you.

MAU   You feel strange.

FATHER   Don't you know your father?

MAU   But if all are dead . . .

FATHER   What are you thinking, Mau?

MAU   I think you are not my father. I think —

FATHER   Yes?

MAU   I think – so many dead —

FATHER   Yes?

MAU   . . .

FATHER   You dare not do it. You dare not
               name me. The fear freezes the word
               on your tongue.

MAU   I do. I know what you are. You're not
               my father. You are Locaha. Stolen his
               body but —

FATHER   Yes.

               Father transforms into Locaha.

LOCAHA   I've come for you.

MAU   I'm not ready.

LOCAHA   Search the island. Nobody left. While
             you lived on the small island, the
             great wave came. Tore deep inside
             them, ripped them of life. No family.
             No Nation. Nobody to tell a story to.
             Nobody to share your food with.
             Better to come with me. Let the sun
             burn you dry. Fall from a high ledge.
             Topple into the lagoon.

MAU   Who am I, with no man ceremony?

LOCAHA   It won't be long. On your own –
             despair. I'll be waiting all the time for
             you. Watching. In a few days, weeks
             at most. You belong to me, little
             Mau.

MAU   We'll see, Locaha.

LOCAHA   I'll hear you.

             Exit Locaha.

MAU   Father. I'm not a man. Or a boy. It's
             hard when everyone you ever know is
             staring at you with no life in them.

             Scream – tribal, ululating.

             Mau prepares his father's body.

MAU   Imo will make you into a dolphin.
             But Imo allowed you to die. Imo is . . .
             Oh. Questions.

Enter Milton.

MAU   What are you? Not an island bird.

MILTON   I can see an island. There'll be people.
               They'll save us. Knickers.

MAU   New words.

MILTON   Everything's emptiness from now on.
               Bottom.

               Exit Milton.

MAU   Must bury them all. This is what a
               man would do. I'm not a man.

               Exit Mau with the body of his father.

THREE

The wreck of the Sweet Judy. *Below deck. Daphne
regains conciousness.*

DAPHNE   Daddy! I had the most terrible dream.
               I—! Hello?

               She finds an oil lamp. Lights it.

               This is Miss Fanshaw. I wonder,
               could one of you gentlemen—

               She sees Roberts.

               Captain Roberts. I have to get to my
               father. He's wait— Oh.

Roberts falls to the floor. He's been dead for a day.

No.

Daphne retches.

Dear God in heaven, don't let me be the only one.

MILTON	(*off*) Let a fellow sleep, can't yer?
DAPHNE	Milton!

Milton enters.

MILTON	I'm ready for my breakfast now.
DAPHNE	Milton. I think everyone died in the storm.
MILTON	Boobies.
DAPHNE	Now how will I get to Daddy?
MILTON	I'm not a man.
DAPHNE	What language is that? Where did you hear that?
MILTON	Someone will help us.
DAPHNE	Show me.

Daphne takes out her telescope and goes on deck as the parrot follows her.

Oh yes. I can see someone. A little speck on the beach. Come on, Milton. Let's introduce ourselves.

MILTON	Ermintrude.
DAPHNE	Don't. I don't like my name.
MILTON	Trudy Fanshaw.
DAPHNE	I don't have to be Ermintrude here.

FOUR

The beach.

MAU	If you made the world. Made us. Why let this happen? Imo? You are cruel. You are hard. I curse you for the rest of my life.

Mau lies down. Silence. Enter Daphne and Milton.

DAPHNE	He looks troubled. What does he see? I've seen people like him in books. The nobbly – I beg your pardon, noble savage. He's a rather marvellous specimen, isn't he? One day I'd like to make a presentation about him to the Royal Society. Maybe Mr Darwin will listen.
MILTON	Nobbly.
DAPHNE	Milton – shhh.
MAU	Agh!

Mau sits up.

DAPHNE   Good morning. I suppose your people
          are local people, yes? My people are
          from Wiltshire. My father is 139th in
          line to the throne. He's Governor of
          Port Mercia. No doubt you've heard
          of that? It's in your hemisphere. I was
          on my way to see him when . . .
          Wasn't the weather absolutely
          shocking?

MAU   Where are your legs?

DAPHNE   So sorry. I don't speak your language.

MAU   What are you? Are you dead?

DAPHNE   Do you speak English?

MAU   Ghost girl.

MILTON   I beg your pardon, nobbly savage.

MAU   Away now. I am Mau. This is my
          Nation.

          *Mau stamps the ground in a ritual
          war chant and then charges forward.*

DAPHNE   No, please don't do that because you
          see I have—

          She produces a gun.

          I really don't want to, but if I have to
          I'll fire.

MAU	What's that stick?
DAPHNE	Keep away from me.
MAU	Never seen one of those before.
DAPHNE	I've warned you and now I'm going to—

Daphne fires. There is a bang but no bullet. Daphne falls backwards, dropping the gun.

MAU	What's this for?

Mau picks up the gun. Points it towards himself and is about to pull the trigger.

DAPHNE	Careful, you mustn't—

At the last moment he turns it around and then pulls trigger.

MAU	Fire. I've got a fire-maker. Thank you.
DAPHNE	I'm sorry I tried to shoot you. I was frightened. I'm so sorry. We haven't been introduced. My name is—
MILTON	Trudy.
DAPHNE	Daphne.
MAU	Daphne. Mau.
MILTON	Mau.
DAPHNE	Mau. A lovely name. Delighted to meet you, Mau.

Daphne extends a hand. Mau copies her.

No. You shake it. Like this.

She shows him.

And then you stop.

MAU	Daphne. My people are dead. Are all your people dead?
DAPHNE	I think maybe, Mau, we are the only ones left alive. But don't worry. Daddy will come. We have to get to know each other. So . . . please – come for tea. (*Mimes.*) At the wreck of the *Sweet Judy*. Tea. (*Mimes.*)
MAU	You want to eat me?
DAPHNE	(*mimes*) There's a little fruit cake and a teapot.
MAU	Are you one of the raiders?
DAPHNE	(*mimes*) Oh I think you think I want to eat you but – no, no, no – I am offering you afternoon tea – over there – in one hour.
MAU	(*mimes*) Alright. Yes.
DAPHNE	If you have any clothes, please wear them when you come for tea. Don't be late. It really is so awfully good to meet you. Let's hope the weather continues fine. Good day.

MILTON   There's a little fruit cake. Now how will I get to Daddy? Delighted to meet you, Mau.

Daphne and Milton exit.

The Grandfathers appear.

G'FATHERS   Mau! Find the God Anchors. Fetch them from the sea and keep the Nation safe.

MAU   But I want to go to see the girl.

G'FATHERS   Half-bake. Don't trust her. Do what the Grandfathers tell you, Mau.

MAU   You? You're just old voices stuck in my head.

G'FATHERS   Beer. Beer. Beer.

MAU   Alright! Beer.

FIVE

The wreck of the Sweet Judy. *Daphne has set up the tea things. She has been waiting a long time for Mau. She takes a telescope and searches for Mau.*

MILTON   Everything's emptiness from now on.

DAPHNE   I want Mau.

MILTON   Mau.

Enter Mau.

DAPHNE   Mau! Well, I must say your time-keeping is very bad. I know you don't have clocks or anything, but I really do think you could have made a little effort. You'll just have to drink your tea cold. One lump or two?

MAU   Daphne. The Grandfathers say: find the God Anchors. Guard the Nation. Watch out for raiders. If I was a man I'd know what to do. See this (*the crab round his neck*)? I'm a crab without a shell lost on the beach.

DAPHNE   I should say two. And a little milk. Like this.

Daphne shows Mau how to drink the tea: she stirs it, then gracefully lifts it to her lips. Mau copies her.

DAPHNE   There's nothing that a cup of tea can't put right, don't you find?

Mau puts down the cup.

Not a tea drinker? I'm sorry, but you seem very sad. Are you sad? (*Mimes.*)

MAU   Yes. Sad.

DAPHNE   I've felt like that for years now. Just me, Grandmother and a huge house. Father had to go away to govern

Port Mercia. But then he sent for me. I'm on my way to . . . I was on my way to . . .

MAU   What? Daphne?

DAPHNE   I may never see home again. No. 'I'll be there when you most need me.' That's what he said and gave me this (*watch*). My father will look for me.

MAU   Daphne.

He reaches out and holds her hand.

DAPHNE   Mau. (*Pause.*) I say, are you going to let go? No? Oh well. I suppose it is rather nice. I say: 'It's very nice, Mau.' Yes. I am happy. (*Mimes.*)

MAU   Happy.

MILTON   Happy.

Two Grandfather Birds appear.

MILTON   What extraordinary fauna.

DAPHNE   These birds . . .

She fetches a book.

MAU   Oh! It opens up. It's like a tattoo but it's better than a tattoo.

DAPHNE   You see – it's a pantaloon bird.

MAU   Pant-a-loon? That's a Grandfather
               Bird. (*Mimes.*) Grandfather.

DAPHNE   Old man? No, it says here—

MAU   My language. My island. My bird.
               Grandfather.

DAPHNE   Alright, since it's your island – old
               man bird. 'Native of the Mothering
               Sunday Islands, a group in the South
               Pelagic.'

MAU   These are the Rising Sun Islands.

DAPHNE   Mau. I would like to give Captain
               Roberts—

MILTON   Oh rapture! Oh everlasting light!

DAPHNE   —a proper burial. He was a very
               Christian man. Will you help me
               to . . .?

MAU   I don't understand you, Daphne.

DAPHNE   Will you. . .

               *Daphne leads Mau around the wreck
               of the* Sweet Judy *to the body of
               Roberts.*

MAU   What is that on his legs?

DAPHNE   Will you help me bury him?

MAU   I will help you, Daphne.

36

DAPHNE   Thank you, Mau.

Mau prepares the body as Grandmother appears.

G'MOTHER   Ermintrude. What is this?

DAPHNE   I'm called Daphne now.

G'MOTHER   I'm sorry, Ermintrude, I didn't hear that.

DAPHNE   I said—

G'MOTHER   Ermintrude, I don't want you running wild with the little native boy.

DAPHNE   He's helping me.

G'MOTHER   I'm catching very little of what you're saying, Ermintrude. Stand up straight. Remember manners and morals at all times.

DAPHNE   Grandmama. Everyone else is dead.

G'MOTHER   No matter. I lost a husband and three children and I never showed a moment's emotion. Back into the shipwreck and study Burke's and Mrs Beeton until you are rescued.

DAPHNE   I'm working with Mau.

G'MOTHER   I strictly forbid you to—

DAPHNE   I'm not listening to you any more.

G'MOTHER	Somebody has to be in charge here. No head man. I will take the lead.
DAPHNE	No.
G'MOTHER	I-I-I-I-I—

Grandmother turns into a bird and flies away.

DAPHNE	The rules are different here.

SIX

The beach. Night time. Mau has folded Roberts' arms. Enter Daphne and Milton. Daphne is in black hat, with a hymn book and a spade. She carries Roberts' captain's hat.

DAPHNE	Good. And now— (*Digs.*) Bury.
MAU	You want to put him in a hole in the ground?
DAPHNE	Yes, that's it.
MILTON	We're all going to be taken.
MAU	We put him in the sea.
DAPHNE	I don't understand you.
MILTON	The rules are different here.
MAU	Out there. Good men become—

Mau and Daphne look out to sea.
Dolphins leap out of the water,
framed against the night sky. They
call to each other and for a brief
moment their cries to each other turn
into a song.

DAPHNE   Yes. Let's put him in the sea and turn
                 him into a dolphin.

MAU   Now we—

                 Mau punctures Roberts' chest with
                 a knife.

DAPHNE   That's horrid.

MILTON   Manners and morals at all times.

MAU   You have to make a hole. Let out his
                 soul.

DAPHNE   Mau – have his hat. It means he was
                 Captain. Now you're head man.

MAU   No, Daphne.

                 Mau puts the hat on the body and
                 chants as he drags Roberts' body into
                 the sea. It floats for a moment and
                 then sinks and is washed away. Mau
                 comes back to Daphne and they look
                 out to sea.

DAPHNE   I want you to have that hat. It's a
                 waste on a dead man.

MAU	You want me to be Chief. I won't be, can't be. I'm just a blue crab.
DAPHNE	I'm going to get it.

Daphne runs into the water.

MAU	The current is strong there, you'll— Daphne!
DAPHNE	I've got it, Mau. I've got the – ah!

She is pulled under the water.

LOCAHA	I have her, Mau. She is mine.
MAU	No.

Mau runs into the water and dives under the waves.

Underwater: Mau swims towards Daphne. She is lifeless.

LOCAHA	Look at her, Mau. No life left. You're alone again. Give in to me. Give me your hand.

Mau grabs Daphne's body and drags her to the surface. She lies still, Roberts' hat in her hand.

MAU	Breathe. Don't let him take you. This. Will. Not. Happen.
DAPHNE	Ahhhhh. I saw a horrible thing. Like death.

MAU   Sleep, Daphne. I'm standing guard.

           *Milton watches as Mau stands guard
           over the sleeping Daphne. Mau
           inspects the hat.*

           Blue crab and chief's hat? What does
           that mean?

MILTON   My language. My island. My bird.

MAU   What's a Nation, Daphne? Are we a
           Nation?

———

SEVEN

*Drums. The Raider Chief enters, surrounded by
several other Raiders. Enter more Raiders, dragging
with them the body of Cox.*

CHIEF   What is this?

RAIDER 1   A gift from the sea.

CHIEF   Is it living?

RAIDER 2   Yes. It is weak but there is a breath.
           What shall we do with it?

CHIEF   Wake it. I will fight it. If it is strong
           we can eat it before tomorrow's raid.

           Cox is woken up.

COX	Come, Miss Ermintrude, it's not a morning to be in bed. I'll open the curtains wide. See the blue sky and the green hills. What a glorious day the Good Lord has sent us.
RAIDER 3	What language is that?
RAIDER 2	Keep away. The sea has spared his life and taken his wits.
COX	Come and play with my boy. He's waiting in the kitchen. Show him your books – the maps of all the countries, names of all the species. Up you get, Miss Ermintrude. Don't keep my boy waiting.
RAIDER 4	What's he talking about?
RAIDER 2	He's talking to phantoms.
COX	'I'm sorry, Bishop. The choir is very much depleted. Over half have the Russian influenza. Miss Mithers passed away at breakfast. I fear others will soon join her in heaven.' 'The Russian influenza's going to kill half the kingdom.' 'Son? Son? What's happening?' 'He's got it too.' 'No. Don't leave us.' 'He's burning up. Russian influenza. My son. I won't lose him. He's all I have. My boy. Boy. Boy. Boy.' 'Take me with you. There's nothing to keep me here since

my . . . I'm head butler. I'll take care of Miss Ermintrude Fanshaw.' 'The coast. The *Sweet Judy*.' 'Why – oh, they're hymning now. Hollow words. What a great dark cloud in my mind.' 'See? Life goes so easy, dun't it? One minute there. Gone. See that dolphin out there on the waves, Miss Fanshaw? Bang. Bang. Bang.' I tried son, did my best. 'Get your revenge. Let out your anger.' That won't make it right. Agggghhh.

CHIEF Half-bake: I challenge you to a fight.

COX Who's that? Who's speaking?

CHIEF I am the Chief of the Raiders and I say: fight.

The Raiders circle around them and there is a ritual of drumming and chanting.

COX A fight, is it? Is that what you want? Well, that's easy. I can win that.

Cox shoots the Raider Chief through the head. He dies instantly. Silence.

RAIDER I He has the soul of Locaha.

COX Got a taste for it now. What's next? Who wants to die?

EIGHT

Evening. Stars. Daphne, Mau and Milton.

DAPHNE   Look. This is my favourite thing.
             Leave Grandmama behind in the
             house. Up onto Duffer's Hill with
             Father and study the stars. Come
             and look.

             *Mau joins her, looks through the
             telescope.*

MAU   They jump close to you. Incredible.

MILTON   Thank goodness the night is so clear.

DAPHNE   Would you like me to teach you their
             names?

MAU   I like your language. It's very beautiful.
             Even when I don't understand you.

DAPHNE   See there? Jup-it-er. Jupiter.

MILTON   Pluto, Saturn, Mars, Venus, Uranus.

MAU   We were told that Imo lived up there.

DAPHNE   I'd like to teach you all about science.

MAU   A boat.

DAPHNE   My father. You see, I told you he'd
             come. Daddy! Daddy! Daddy!

MAU   Daphne. No. I'm sorry.

DAPHNE

I want my daddy.

On the beach below, Ataba enters.
Enter Mau.

ATABA

Boy. Go and fetch your Chief. Tell
him we are here. Most on our island
are dead. We few survived the wave.

MAU

Sir—

ATABA

Go, boy. Fast.

MAU

But sir—

ATABA

Do not question me. I am high priest
Ataba. Tell your Chief—

MAU

Sir. Ataba. We have no Chief. I am all
that is left of the Nation.

ATABA

All gone? But this is our biggest
island. I trained as a priest here. The
island of the God Anchors. Surely—

MAU

Nothing.

ATABA

Then who is to help us?

MAU

I will do my best. And there's—

Enter Daphne and Milton.

ATABA

Ugh! Half-bake.

MAU

Waggle her hand.

MILTON

No bloody way. You're bad luck.

ATABA	Made from bad clay before Imo worked out how to make real people. Look. Crying.
DAPHNE	I'm so sorry. I— I— hoped you were someone else.

Enter Milo and Pilu, supporting Cahle, who is only an hour away from giving birth.

MILO	Help us. My woman is about to have a baby. Tell the Chief and have the women prepare for her. Everything must be ready.
MAU	But . . . there is no Chief. There are no women.
MILO	Has this one had the woman ceremony?
CAHLE	Aaaaaahhhhhhhhhhhhhhhhhhh!
PILU	(*to Daphne*) You must deliver child.
DAPHNE	You speak English.
PILU	Year I live Port Mercia.
MILTON	'I'll be there when you most need me.'
DAPHNE	Did you meet my father? He's the Governor of Port . . .
MILO	No time for this, Pilu. She must be taken to the women's place.

DAPHNE   Please. Tell me about my father.

PILU   Your father is good man and he tells of daughter who—

MILO   You will deliver child.

PILU   He says you must— (*Indicates.*)

DAPHNE   But I can't, I'm only—

MILO   You must.

PILU   That is way here. Men wait outside.

DAPHNE   But I don't know how.

MILO   You will be told. Woman's wisdom.

PILU   (*to the others*) She will deliver the baby.

ATABA   Let a half-bake touch a baby?

MILO   It is the only way. Quick. Up to the women's place.

Cable is being taken up to the women's place, Pilu pushes Daphne after her.

DAPHNE   Mau – (*Mimes.*) There's a medical book in the shipwreck. Bring that.

MAU   What does she say?

PILU   Bring medicine bag and book from ship. It won't do any good.

47

MAU   I'll fetch it.

Milo, Pilu, Cahle and Daphne head off to the women's place. Mau runs off to the wreck.

ATABA   Where are the God Anchors? They're missing.

MILTON   Silence. You bugger.

NINE

The women's place. Daphne and Cahle are inside a straw hut. Outside Milo and Pilu are waiting.

DAPHNE   Now if you lie down. Or squat. Yes. Whichever is most appropriate.

Mau pushes the book through the entrance to the hut.

Here's the medical book which will tell us . . . (*Looks.*) Except it's for sailors and so it's all about cutting off legs and about . . . Oh . . . there's nothing – nothing – nothing here to show me how to do this. Stupid book.

Throws the book aside.

I've never seen a birth. My mother . . . She was in such pain. I heard that from the other end of the house. And when she stopped screaming I thought the baby was born but they were. . .

She goes out of the hut.

PILU   What you doing?

DAPHNE   I can't.

MAU   Are you sad, Daphne?

MILO   You can't leave her alone. That's my woman.

MAU   Don't give them to Locaha. Do you understand me, Daphne? I don't have your words but. This. Will. Not. Happen.

DAPHNE   But I'm frightened I can't . . . I understand you, Mau. This will not happen.

          Daphne goes back into the hut.

          I'm going to work this out. I'll make sure that you and your baby live.

          Daphne begins to deliver the baby.

PILU   Is child coming?

DAPHNE   Yes.

          The birth continues.

MILO   Naming.

PILU   You must sing a naming song.

MILO   Bad luck if you don't.

PILU   Bad luck if you don't.

DAPHNE   Oh! Er . . .

Twinkle twinkle little star
How I wonder what you are
Up above the world so high
Like a diamond in the sky.

MILO   Has she named the child?

PILU   Twinkull.

MILO   Twink-ull.

MAU   It's good.

PILU   She says it will shine as brightly as the stars above us.

Cahle reaches out and Daphne gives her the baby.

CAHLE   You did very well.

DAPHNE   He's beautiful.

CAHLE   He's beautiful. What do I do now? Do I feed him? Don't know what to do. What do we do when there are no grandmothers to guide us?

DAPHNE   You look tired.

CAHLE   He is so beautiful but I am so weak. How will I ever care for him?

DAPHNE	Sleep now.
	Daphne comes out of the hut.
DAPHNE	It's a boy.
PILU	It's a boy.
MILO	Yay! Twink-ull, Twink-ull, Twink-ull!
PILU	See. Woman's wisdom. You know what to do.
MAU	Daphne. You were wonderful.
	He kisses her.
DAPHNE	Mau. Don't do that. It's not altogether appropriate.
MAU	What did she say?
PILU	She said she liked it and you should kiss her again.
MAU	Right.
	Mau kisses Daphne again.
DAPHNE	Mau! I'm going to wash myself in the sea.
	Daphne runs off.
MAU	Er?
PILU	She said: chase her and catch her.
MAU	Ha!

Mau runs off.

MILO   Twink-ull. Look up at the stars. They
              are yours. Everything in this world
              sings welcome to you.

————

TEN

————

*The next day. Bright sun. A clearing. Enter Mau
followed by Ataba.*

MAU   I tell you what I think. We don't need
              the God Anchors.

ATABA   Mau!

MAU   The God Anchors were in their place
              when the wave came and what did
              that mean? Nothing. They're just bits
              of stone that we believe keep us safe.

ATABA   Don't anger the gods, Mau. Imo is
              listening.

MAU   I say: shit on the gods. Shit on Imo
              who can allow a Nation to—

ATABA   What are you? Neither boy-soul or
              man-soul. You're not a Chief. You're
              not even Mau. You're a demon.

MAU   Shut up, old man. There are no
              demons, no gods. Just me. And the
              waves and the sun and birth and

52

death. And there's no reason for
anything.

Enter Milo and Cahle with Twinkle.

MILO   Quick. Help. Cahle. Twink-ull.

*Mau and Ataba run after Milo and
arrive at the beach at the same time
as Pilu and Daphne. Cahle is sitting
and is holding up the baby and
keening.*

DAPHNE   What is it?

PILU   She can't feed baby. Twinkle very
                weak.

*Cahle holds out the baby to Daphne,
who takes it.*

DAPHNE   Twinkle. It's like he can't see anything.

CAHLE   I'm no mother. These breasts are dry.
                Wish I was dead.

MILO   No, woman.

PILU   He must milk or dead tomorrow.

MAU   Daphne. (*Mimes.*) I'll hold the baby
                while you prepare your breasts for
                feeding.

DAPHNE   No! You have to be married.

MILTON   . . .

PILU   Mau – she's too young. Her breasts
                don't make milk.

MAU   What can we do for Twink-ull?

PILU   Nothing.

CAHLE   Aaaaaaahhh!

                She grabs the child from Daphne.

ATABA   We will ask Imo to watch over him as
                he dies and see that Locaha makes
                him into a dolphin as soon as his
                spirit leaves his body.

                *Everyone kneels, Daphne included,
                although she doesn't really know
                what is going on. Ataba starts to
                chant. Pilu takes Twinkle and places
                him on the ground as though a ritual
                to mark the beginning of the baby's
                death is about to begin.*

DAPHNE   I wish I was a woman. I wish I had
                breasts to make milk. I wish I was—
                What can we do, Mau? Think of
                something. Will. Not. Happen.

MAU   I – I – I – YES! Make beer.

PILU   We can't feed the baby beer.

MAU   No – it's not for the— I know what
                to do – there's no time. I'll get milk
                for you – make beer.

MILO	What are you doing?
MAU	Do as I say. Stop that now, old man. I have a plan.
ALL	No!

A beer ceremony. Milo fetches a fruit which is something between a coconut and a melon. Meanwhile Pilu fetches an axe to chop open the fruit. Cahle brings a bowl from which the juice of the fruit can be poured. Ataba begins a percussive sequence.

Once the juice is in the bowl, everyone comes forward one at a time to spit in the bowl. Daphne is embarrassed to do this, but Mau encourages her. Now they all sing – Daphne trying to join in.

ALL
What have you done son?
What have you done?
Why is your brother so still?

Travel far enough you meet yourself
Travel long enough you'll be home.

Father, forgive me, we had a fight
I hunted, he was my kill.

Travel far enough you'll meet yourself
Travel long enough you'll be home.

Never return son, never return
Travel and never come home.

> Travel far enough you'll meet yourself
> Travel long enough you'll be home.

> Father, I wandered, now I am old
> Travelled so far I am home.

> Travel far enough you'll meet yourself
> Travel long enough you'll be home.

MILO   The beer is ready.

Mau picks up the bowl of beer, then grabs Daphne's hand.

MAU   Wait on the beach. I'll get milk for you. Come.

DAPHNE   Where are we going?

Mau leads Daphne deep into the forest.

MAU   Look!

A huge sow is there with her piglets suckling.

DAPHNE   (*mimes*) That's no use.

MAU   It's all we've got.

DAPHNE   (*mimes*) You can milk a cow and a goat but a pig you can't – no udders.

MAU   There are other ways.

Mau moves towards sow.

DAPHNE   Careful, she'll attack.

MAU   Come, Mother Pig. There's beer for
              you. Drink.

              The sow begins to drink the beer.

              *Mau grabs a pile of dirt and starts to
              rub it over Daphne.*

DAPHNE   Ugh!

MILTON   The Wiltshire Fanshaws.

              *Mau rubs himself with mud and
              moves towards the sow, acting like
              a piglet. The sow snores.*

DAPHNE   Are you watching, Grandmama? You
              should look away.

              *Daphne turns into a piglet rolling in
              mud and approaches the sow with
              Mau.*

MAU   And now we—

              Mau goes to suck.

DAPHNE   Oh yuck. That is the most disgusting
              thing I've ever—

MAU   You want Twinkle to live? Then you
              do this or Locaha—

DAPHNE   Yes, Mau. I understand. I can. I will.

MAU   Imagine it's your mother.

DAPHNE   What?

MAU   Just do it.

                 *Daphne and Mau both feed alongside
                 the other piglets. Mau produces a
                 container for them to spit the milk
                 into.*

MAU   That's it. Come on.

                 Mau leads Daphne back to the others.

MAU   Here. Feed him now.

                 Cahle feeds Twinkle.

CAHLE   Oh, Twinkle. Hungry. He likes it.

PILU   He happy now.

MAU   See, old man. No need to die.

DAPHNE   (*to Mau*) You smell disgusting.

PILU   She says you a pig.

MAU   Pig too.

                 Daphne and Mau laugh and play pigs.

                 Enter Milton.

MILTON   (*snorting noises*) Worms! Help!

                 *From the forest, about twenty very
                 undernourished Islanders appear. An
                 Islander comes forward.*

ISLANDER   Please help us. Our homes were
                 destroyed by the wave. We've been

wandering the seas looking for others. We made our way here to the big island. Everyone has heard of the Nation. We don't have anything to offer you except our hunger. Will you turn us away or will you share your Nation? Who decides? Who is Chief here?

MAU　　There is no Chief.

PILU　　Mau is Chief.

ATABA　　No.

MILO　　This is Mau's island. He is the oldest man from the Nation still living. He is Chief.

ATABA　　He doubts the gods.

PILU　　Still. He is the only one. Mau. You must decide. Do we share the food and land of your island with these strangers? Mau!

MAU　　I'm not ready. I can't carry the burden. What do the Grandfathers want?

ATABA　　Yes. We must pray to the ancestors before we know.

Marisgala, very old and weak, comes forward but stumbles and falls. Daphne runs to her.

DAPHNE	This woman. She's dying. Why aren't you helping?
CAHLE	Decide.
MAU	No more death. I'm Mau.
PILU	And he is Chief.
MAU	And . . . I'm Chief.
MILTON	Arses.
ATABA	A blue crab?
MAU	Come and join us. We are the Nation.

Marisgala, supported by Daphne, and her group come forward.

	We must build shelters to keep off the sun and the rain.
DAPHNE	There are hammers, saws, ropes we can use on the *Sweet Judy*.
PILU	She offers tools.
DAPHNE	And medicines.
PILU	We must build fences to keep out the pigs. We must grow crops to feed our people.
DAPHNE	(*to Marisgala, miming*) I will feed you now.

MAU   We don't have enough.

DAPHNE   There's food on the *Sweet Judy*. Rum
            and biscuits mostly, but—

PILU   Everyone, we will have a feast of
            trouserman food.

MAU   May every day be as happy as this
            one.

            They sing as barrels of Sweet Judy
            *food and rum are fetched. Tools are
            passed around.*

ELEVEN

*Drumming. Enter Polegrave and Foxlip, led on by a
group of Raiders.*

FOXLIP   We are subjects of His Majesty the
            King of England and all the Empire.
            If you harm us—

POLEGRAVE   Hands off, darkie.

FOXLIP   We will make war on you with our
            navy and our cannons and you will
            be blown away.

POLEGRAVE   Let me get my gun.

RAIDER   Silence. Here comes the Chief.

More drums. Cox enters. He is now the Raider Chief.

COX   Bring them closer.

POLEGRAVE   It's the butler man.

FOXLIP   Cox!

POLEGRAVE   Mr Cox?

FOXLIP   Remember us?

RAIDER   What should we do with them, Chief?

POLEGRAVE   Must remember. The *Sweet Judy*. The big wave. We—

COX   Silence. I am Chief here.

FOXLIP   You don't even speak their language. English same as us.

COX   Death is everything here. Everything is Death. This is where I belong.

POLEGRAVE   You must remember—

COX   What happened to the girl?

POLEGRAVE   Miss Fanshaw?

FOXLIP   Drowned with all the rest.

COX   But did you see it? Did you see the life go out of her?

FOXLIP   No but—

COX	I have to be sure. My boy was taken and I want her – kid for a kid. That's only fair, isn't it? Can't rest until I'm sure that Miss Fanshaw is dead.

Cox bites at Polegrave's arm.

	Bad meat. Make them slaves.
FOXLIP	We're no slaves. Englishmen.
COX	Slave. Hard life. Short life. More life than many have. Away

Exeunt with drums.

TWELVE

Heavy rain. Mau is standing guard on the beach. He now wears Roberts' hat and trousers, and carries an umbrella. Enter Milo.

MAU	I'll watch until the sun is high.
MILO	You've been here for a day.
MAU	I'm Chief. I should watch out for raiders.
MILO	But not all the time. Sometimes others—
MAU	Don't question me. How are the new huts?

MILO   Not so good.

MAU   They need more work.

MILO   The rains are so bad.

MAU   Milo . . . what do the Nation say
                about me?

MILO   They say . . . you are liked.

MAU   Yes?

MILO   Some of them laugh at you – the
                things you took from the wreck –
                your trouserman clothes.

MAU   Savages. These hold tools. This keeps
                off the rain. It's progress.

MILO   And some say you are a boy and
                don't know how to see us through the
                rains. That we'll starve and our
                homes will be washed away.

MAU   Who says so? I'll fight them if I must.
                I'm strong. The strongest.

                *Enter a group of Islanders, who kneel
                before Mau. One of them comes
                forward.*

ISLANDER 1   Chief. For so many moons, it has
                rained. Our food is running out. We
                sleep on wet ground. Yesterday a hut
                was washed away.

MAU   Then we must build stronger huts.

Islander 2 comes forward.

ISLANDER 2   Chief. The gods are not pleased with
             us. The Nation has no God Anchors.
             Without God Anchors we have no
             protection. We must—

MAU   But it's not the God Anchors who say
             whether the rain falls or the—

ISLANDER 3   Chief. We live in fear. We have no
             hope. If we can look to the beach and
             see the three God Anchors—

MAU   The weather comes whatever man
             does. Do you believe in the God
             Anchors?

ISLANDER 3   Always.

Enter Ataba and Pilu.

ATABA   Are you bringing back the God
             Anchors?

MAU   Yes. I am.

ATABA   You're a great Chief.

MAU   People are foolish. I must do
             whatever I can to stop their fear.
             Fetch the canoe. We'll sail into the
             lagoon.

ATABA   I'll come with you.

MAU	Just Milo and Pilu.
ATABA	But the High Priest must be there when the God Anchors return.
MAU	If you like.

Enter Daphne and Cahle, carrying Twinkle. Daphne has shed much of her Victorian clothing and is now wearing her undergarments with a grass skirt on top, plus an umbrella to keep off the rain.

MAU	You look different, Daphne.
DAPHNE	(*mimes*) Are you going beyond the lagoon?
MAU	It looks good. Yes. (*Mimes.*) We're going far out.
DAPHNE	Please take care.

Daphne hugs Mau, who exits with Pilu, Milo and Atabar.

DAPHNE	(*mimes*) Are there sharks in the water?
CAHLE	(*nods*) Sometimes.
DAPHNE	Oh.

Twinkle cries, Cahle comforts him.

DAPHNE	Cahle. My brother only lived a few hours. My brother. They buried them

separately. Two coffins. My mother in a box and beside her another tiny . . . Why did they do that? Why didn't they bury them together? They should have. . .

CAHLE   I don't understand.

DAPHNE   (*mimes*) I'm going to say a prayer for Mau. Will you join me?

Cahle shakes head.

I know you don't believe in my god. I'm not sure I believe in my god, but still . . .

Daphne kneels in prayer. Cahle joins her, still holding Twinkle.

DAPHNE   If anyone is listening. Keep Mau safe.

THIRTEEN

A canoe crosses the lagoon. Mau is at the front, guiding. Pilu and Milo are rowing. Ataba is at the back of the boat.

Mau indicates when they've reached a particular spot. He dives into the water and finds the first God Anchor. It has a large hand on it, holding a set of compasses. Once, he's located it, Milo and Pilu join him and together they bring the God Anchor back to the surface and into the boat.

They move on and repeat this process with the second God Anchor. This one has a horse on it.

Then Mau dives down for the third God Anchor. He comes back up.

MAU	There are two more God Anchors down there.
ATABA	Impossible.
MAU	That's what I saw.
ATABA	Everyone knows there are only three anchors.
MAU	Then maybe everyone is wrong. I'll fetch them.
ATABA	No. Everyone believes in three anchors.
MAU	But if that's not the truth—
ATABA	It is what we believe.
MAU	Old man!

Mau dives below the water.

ATABA	No!

Ataba pursues Mau below the water. Mau is right. There are two more stones. Ataba struggles with Mau. Ataba's foot is cut. Blood fills the water. Mau drags Ataba to the surface.

MAU	Take him back to the Nation. He's bleeding badly.
MILO	But Mau—
MAU	Do it now.
PILU	There's blood in the water. Sharks—
MAU	I'm going back for the God Anchors. When the people see there are more stones than the priests told them—
MILO	It's too dangerous, Mau.
MAU	Do as your Chief says.
ATABA	(*weak*) Mau—
MAU	I'm not listening to you, old man.
ATABA	Remember this: if a shark attacks . . .

Mau leans in close to hear as Ataba, too weak to talk any more loudly, mumbles in his ear.

MAU	Goodbye.

Milo and Pilu reluctantly row Ataba back to the island.

Mau dives back into the bloodied water.

He pulls at a God Anchor, but a shark comes towards him.

The shark is very close, its jaws open to consume Mau.

Locaha appears.

LOCAHA   I'm waiting for you.

MAU   Locaha!

LOCAHA   Ataba told you: swim towards it and
           shout as loud as you can. He's an old
           man who believes in gods and stones
           and—

MAU   It's the only thing I have.

           *Mau swims towards the shark and
           shouts: a huge noise that we hear as
           from the shark's perspective. The
           shark retreats.*

MAU   Did it!

LOCAHA   But still, Mau, I will take you. You let
           in too much water. Drowned in the
           lagoon. You're mine.

           Mau loses consciousness.

FOURTEEN

*Night. Pilu and Milo bring Mau's body on to the
beach. Several members of the Nation, including
Cahle with Twinkle, are waiting for them.*

CAHLE   How is he?

MILO   He has only a little breath now.

CAHLE	Will he live?
MILO	I don't think so.

Daphne comes rushing on with the ship's medicine bag.

DAPHNE	Mau.
CAHLE	No, Daphne.
PILU	She can use white medicine.
CAHLE	There's nothing you can do.
DAPHNE	But I must.

Daphne pushes through to Mau and kneels by his body with stethoscope.

DAPHNE   You see, if you understand science then everything is possible. With science the most incredible things can be achieved. And if we only apply . . . There you see, a little breath – and all we need to do is . . . His heart is beating – so there's hope – we must hope – breath, heart, a pulse, a . . . There's no pulse – his – Mau! Mau! Please don't— No. Mau, it's Daphne. There must be a rational . . . Oh, there's no breath, no heart, no—

The rest of the Nation arrive, including Ataba, who is very weak and being supported.

PILU   The Chief is dead.

ALL   The Chief is dead.

CAHLE   He was a great Chief.

DAPHNE   He's too young.

MILO   He must be given the greatest honour.

MARISGALA The High Priest must agree.

PILU   Ataba?

ATABA   He was a wise chief. Take him to the cave of the grandfathers.

DAPHNE   He can't be. He must—

ATABA   Silence, half-bake. He is going now.

DAPHNE   He can't be. Will not happen.

Marisgala comes forward.

MARISGALA There is a way.

ATABA   No.

DAPHNE   What does she say?

MARISGALA If you take a drop of the root of the—

PILU   That's a superstition. It won't work.

DAPHNE   What is it?

MARISGALA I know how to make the spell. I can send the girl down to fight Locaha.

ATABA   No witchcraft.

DAPHNE	Does she know a way?
MILO	You would just kill her too.
MARISGALA	Or maybe she would save Mau.
DAPHNE	Mau? Mau can live? Tell me.
PILU	Woman give you poison. You die for moment. You go down to Locaha. Mau is journeying to him now. You bring Mau back. But it dangerous. One drop of poison. One drop of antidote. Could kill you.
MILO	Have you ever seen this work?
MARISGALA	The grandmothers—
ATABA	Old wives' tales.
DAPHNE	I'll do it.
CAHLE	No, Daphne.
MARISGALA	Brave girl.
ATABA	Foolish girl. Wicked old woman.
MARISGALA	Prepare her for the journey. Lay her beside Mau.
DAPHNE	I'm going to fight Locaha. This will not happen.

A ritual: Daphne and Mau are laid out side by side as the Nation sing and move around them. Marisgala produces a small container of poison.

MARISGALA   Locaha, we challenge you. Locaha, we send a brave one into your world from which few return. Locaha – she comes and we wish for her return. Now drink.

Daphne drinks the poison.

First you will heat in your body, then great cold.

Daphne's body goes into spasm as several of the Nation hold her.

CAHLE   You've killed her.

MARISGALA   Maybe. And now she has until this drop of antidote reaches her lips to find Mau in the land of Locaha. The drop begins to fall.

Marisgala dips her finger into the pot of antidote and a single drop begins to fall towards Daphne's mouth . . .

FIFTEEN

Daphne appears in absolute emptiness.

DAPHNE   Mau!

Locaha appears, everywhere and nowhere.

LOCAHA   I have him. Go back or I will take you too.

DAPHNE   I've come here for Mau.

LOCAHA   He's at peace. Let him rest.

DAPHNE   That's a lie. He's not ready. Mau, Mau. This will not happen.

Mau runs towards her.

MAU   Run, Daphne.

LOCAHA   Run for ever?

MAU   If we have to.

Daphne and Mau start running. A shoal of dream fish appear.

MAU   Dream fish. Swim through them.

They run into the fish. One gets into Daphne's hair.

DAPHNE   It's in my hair.

MAU   Get it out. Quick.

DAPHNE   I can't.

A hall in an ancient island city, busy with Islanders.

A telescope of a very non-European design. Islanders gather around it.

The Islanders are dancing and singing. Mau joins them.

LOCAHA   Somewhere on the other side of the world – (*to Daphne*) your side of the world – ice plains are melting and soon – the waters rise and—

DAPHNE   This is the past. Leave. All of you. Your world is in danger.

LOCAHA   No one believes the mad girl.

DAPHNE   There's a great wave coming.

LOCAHA   Crazy ghost girl. 'The sky is falling!'

The Islanders laugh and dance.

LOCAHA   Who will ever believe that their world will be washed away? Save your breath.

MAU   It's coming. The great—

A huge wave floods the room and wipes away the whole island civilization.

LOCAHA   All of them are mine. They are Locaha and now you are Locaha—

MAU   No.

DAPHNE   Run!

They run again, into a void.

Marisgala appears faintly.

76

DAPHNE   We're coming. We've made it, Mau.
              We're nearly—

MARISGALA   Not yet, Daphne.

              *A Victorian funeral cortège has
              appeared. Father and Grandmother
              are at the head. There are two coffins:
              one for Daphne's mother and a very
              small one for her baby brother.*

MAU   Daphne?

G'MOTHER   Arnold, I can see a tear.

FATHER   That's right, Mother. You can. I'm
              crying. I've lost a wife and a son.

G'MOTHER   Remember. You're 139th in line to
              the throne.

              *The Choir sings as the coffins are
              lowered into the ground.*

CHOIR   Guide us Lord through vales of
                  darkness
              Give our hearts the strength to bear
              Suffering and deepest sorrow.
              Black is night and dawn comes slowly
              Shine your light eternally.

              *Daphne rushes forward to the coffins
              as the choir breaks off.*

DAPHNE   They should be together. Not the
              little baby alone. Open this one up

and put him in with Mother. Please! Open it!

Daphne grabs at the coffin lid. She is pulled away.

G'MOTHER   Ermintrude!

COX   Come, Miss. Your mother and brother are gone. They'll be safe in God's hands. Boy. You look to Miss Ermintrude.

SON   Yes, Dad.

Cox restrains Daphne as Locaha grabs Mau.

MAU   Daphne.

Cahle, Pilu, Milo and Marisgala appear.

MILO   You've killed them both.

MARISGALA   No. If she is a brave woman, then—

They disappear.

DAPHNE   Not two coffins. I'll—

Daphne tears at her brother's coffin lid. She stops, too scared to go on.

Daphne takes off the coffin lid.

Daphne picks up the dead baby.

She holds the baby to her as she pulls the lid off her mother's coffin.

Daphne puts the baby into her mother's arms.

MOTHER   Thank you.

Light streams out of the coffin, bleaching everything to white.

SIXTEEN

Daphne and Mau are side by side with Marisgala, Ataba, Cahle, Twinkle, Milo and Pilu watching over them.

MARISGALA   She's back.

CAHLE   Yes!

MARISGALA   Only the strongest and bravest women return from the land of Locaha.

ATABA   This is a strong woman.

DAPHNE   Mau – are you . . . ?

MARISGALA   He's back too, Daphne. Look.

MAU   Where did I . . . ?

DAPHNE   Oh Mau.

MAU   Tired.

ATABA   Let the Nation take care of itself for
              a day. Sleep.

              *Mau sleeps. Exit Cahle, Twinkle,
              Milo, Pilu and Ataba.*

DAPHNE   Did he see the same things as me?
              Was that dreaming?

MARISGALA   Look Daphne. Dream fish.

              *Marisgala takes the dream fish from
              her hair. It fills the world with light.*

DAPHNE   That was real. What does it . . . does
              it . . .?

              *Marisgala indicates the open mouth
              of the cave of the Grandfathers.*

              Daphne gets up and looks into cave.

              What does it mean?

ECHO   What does it mean?

              *Daphne steps into the mouth of the
              cave.*

              Mau turns in his sleep.

DAPHNE   (*calls from inside cave*) Mau! Wake
              up! You have to see what's inside
              here!

              *Mau snores. Daphne comes back to
              Mau.*

DAPHNE   Mau.

MARISGALA   Not yet.

DAPHNE   But I have to tell him what's inside.

MARISGALA   Such impatience. There will come a day when you will need to tell him. You'll know when it comes. Not now. Sleep. Together. That's it. Just hold him and sleep.

Marisgala watches Mau and Daphne sleep. Enter Milton.

MILTON   The land. The skies. So many questions. But we are making answers.

End of Act One.

Act Two

ONE

A year later.

The God Anchors stand in a circle.

A group of native women are rehearsing a dance to a tune which sounds suspiciously like 'Happy Birthday'.

Daphne stands high up and lets out a great ululating cry.

Enter the Nation, which now numbers about forty people. Finally enter Mau, Milton, Cahle and Milo with Twinkle.

MAU   People of the Nation. Milo, Cahle, Twinkle. Today is a very special day. One summer has passed since our first birth. On that day Twinkle came into the world, was named and so today we say—

ATABA   May the gods bless your birth festival. Air.

Enter Islanders playing Air. He carries a stone globe, has a huge stomach and four sons on his shoulders.

See his sons around him? Water.

Enter 'Water', also carrying a stone globe.

See how brilliant she is? Save your daughters from fire. Bind him.

Enter 'Fire', hands tied to his side and a glittering red globe on his head.

Above them all: Imo.

Enter 'Imo'.

The gods are happy for you.

Cheer. Daphne leads the women. They sing the English words but accompany it with an island dance of gestures.

WOMEN   Happy birthday to you,
Happy birthday to you,
Happy birthday, dear Twinkle,
Happy birthday to you.

MARISGALA   (*presenting the spear*) May you be a great warrior, Twinkle.

DAPHNE   He's only one.

MARISGALA   Every boy must – (*Stabbing motion.*)

The other women laugh and show their approval.

DAPHNE   This is a new Nation. We don't have to do things the same as before.

Maybe he won't want to be a warrior.
Maybe he'd like to, I don't know, be
a weaver . . .

The women's laughter is getting louder.

Or maybe stay on the island and
collect herbs – oh, stop laughing at
me.

MARISGALA   When you have your own child, then
you'll see. When you and Mau—

DAPHNE   Twinkle, if you choose, may you be a
great . . .

*She blanks, then thinks of something
and hands over her father's fob
watch.*

May you be a great scientist.

MILO   What's this?

CAHLE   It's got bits that move. He likes that,
don't you, Twinkle?

TWINKLE   Yeah.

*Everyone gathers round to look at
the watch – passing it around,
playing with it. Mau takes Daphne
aside.*

MAU   Your father's watch.

MILTON   'Don't worry, Daddy will come.'

DAPHNE	It's been two years. I think if he hasn't come by now . . .
MAU	You don't want to go back to Great Britain and attend lectures at the Royal Society?
DAPHNE	Maybe I'll be here for ever.
MAU	Would you like to be here for ever?
MILTON	'His heart is beating – so there's hope—'
MAU	Look at them. Savages. They're looking in wonder at something you take for granted.
DAPHNE	But that's not the entire—
MAU	And the God Anchors. What are the pictures on the stone? What do they show?
DAPHNE	I don't know.
MAU	You know. Why don't you tell them? Why don't you tell the savages what they are? TELL THEM!

Mau's anger has attracted the attention of the Islanders, who now gather round him and the God Anchors.

ATABA	Mau, why are you so angry?
MAU	Because we are so worthless, because . . . this is Twinkle's day but the world

he's living in . . . This is not our world.

DAPHNE   Stop this.

MAU   Why are we alive? Because we made shelters with tools from *her* boat. How did we survive before the crops grew? Because we ate her rations. She speaks our language now, but we live in her world.

ATABA   Enough. Be proud. Imo made us first before all other men.

MAU   Imo? His God Anchors? Hah! What are these pictures? Come on. Tell us. What's this one?

He grabs Daphne and walks her up to the God Anchors.

MAU   Tell them.

DAPHNE   They're called callipers.

MAU   This one?

DAPHNE   A horse.

MAU   You think they're sacred signs. These are white men's things. Old man – your God Anchors. Bits of stone left behind when white men paid a call generations ago.

PILU   Mau!

ATABA   Daphne? Is this true? Are these not
             our God Anchors?

MAU   Old man . . .

ATABA   Have we been so foolish all these
             years?

MAU   No. Not foolish.

ATABA   So. We are nothing? So proud. So
             stupid. Live amongst the remnants of
             a greater race?

DAPHNE   No. That isn't so. We don't need –
             this.

             *Daphne grabs the watch and throws
             it onto the ground.*

TWINKLE   Present. (*Cries.*)

             *Daphne stamps on the watch,
             breaking it.*

MILTON   I must say your timekeeping is very
             bad.

DAPHNE   (*to Marisgala*) This is the time.

MARISGALA   You're right.

DAPHNE   (*to Mau.*) It's not as it seems. You're
             wrong. I can see why you . . . But no.

CAHLE   Shhh, Twinkle.

DAPHNE   Everyone, open the cave of the
             grandfathers.

ATABA	No!
DAPHNE	The answer is inside.
MAU	Do as she says. Do it!
DAPHNE	That night you were sleeping after the shark, Locaha . . . I saw . . . I thought I was dreaming but I wasn't. Ever since I've been thinking. And I know that was real. Let me show you.

TWO

The Nation follow Daphne up the hill. The rock in the entrance to the cave is rolled open.

ATABA	Only great Chiefs who are dead can go into the cave.
MILTON	Oh Mau! Wake up! You have to see what's inside here!
ATABA	You went inside? Blasphemer.
DAPHNE	Come on, please. This is the great secret of your people.
MAU	We will go inside.
MILTON	Wasn't the weather absolutely shocking?
MAU	No parrot.

MILTON	Arses.

Mau, Daphne and Ataba enter the mouth of the cave. It's dark inside. Mau lights a lamp.

The Grandfathers stretch out before them, wrapped in papervine. They move slightly.

ATABA	The Grandfathers forbid us to do this.
MAU	They are wrapped in papervine. The heat stretches the papervine. It makes them move. It's alright.

They move forward into the darkness.

DAPHNE	How many times do you put a Grandfather in here?
ATABA	Once in a generation.
DAPHNE	See how many there are?
MAU	There are thousands. What does this prove?
DAPHNE	That this cave has been here thousands and thousands of years. That you've had the grandfather ceremony for—
MAU	That we've been savages for a long time?
ATABA	The gods!

*Suddenly there appear four huge
statues of Air, Fire, Water and Imo,
very like the 'masqueraders' at
Twinkle's birthday.*

ATABA   We have reached the home of the
           gods. Can you doubt me now? They
           are here. I see them. Imo – while
           others doubted, I always worshipped
           you.

           Ataba falls prostrate.

MAU   They're statues, old man. Maybe the
           white men left them too.

DAPHNE   No. Count the Grandfathers. Too
           many thousands of years. These have
           been here since . . . White men didn't
           have boats. Europe was under an ice
           cap. These are your statues.

ATABA   I see the gods.

MAU   They're stone.

ATABA   Who says the gods are made of flesh?

MAU   Daphne – when I look through your
           telescope, I see the planets. The one
           you call Jupiter. It has four moons
           that race around it. Like the Air God
           here with his four sons who race
           around their father.

DAPHNE   What are you thinking, Mau?

MAU   And the Fire God – here. His hands were tied to stop him stealing her daughters. Through the telescope I saw what you call Saturn. It has rings.

DAPHNE   Yes.

MAU   Daphne—

DAPHNE   Yes?

MAU   Can it be possible?

DAPHNE   It is. Say it. Tell yourself what you see.

MAU   Daphne – so many thousands of years ago my people saw the stars as close as you see the stars – and we made them into gods?

DAPHNE   Yes!

MAU   Yes! But. How can savages see the stars so close?

DAPHNE   Look at the gods. See why they're shining.

ATABA   That is Imo's light. Don't touch divinity. It will burn.

DAPHNE   Come and look.

Mau touches Imo.

MAU   This is 'glass'. Like in your telescope.

DAPHNE	Yes. While we were still under ice, you made glass.
PILU	Impossible!
DAPHNE	Proof. Touch it. Your people once made glass. And here – gold. With glass and metal you can make lenses. We call them spectacles—
MAU	And telescopes.
DAPHNE	You could study the stars.
MAU	Is this true?
DAPHNE	And here are the – look – your star charts.

They move further and a great wall appears, embedded with glass to make a map of the night sky.

MAU	Glass too. This is our work?
DAPHNE	You must be the oldest civilization in the world.
ATABA	I told you: Imo made us first and then the trousermen with the left-over clay. She admits. Imo be praised!
MAU	Incredible.
DAPHNE	You looked at the stars. And you travelled the world. Here.

A great long line of stones with carvings on are discovered.

MAU   Look, old man. There's more than three. Hundreds of God Anchors.

DAPHNE   You saw the world and recorded it on the stones.

ATABA   Imo's mysteries are infinite.

MAU   'Travel far enough you'll meet yourself Travel far enough you'll be home.'

The song means we moved around the world.

DAPHNE   Yes!

MAU   And we put our journeys, discoveries, knowledge onto these stones.

DAPHNE   Your university. Your museum. Your planetarium. Your city.

MAU   And we forgot all this? We became savages.

DAPHNE   Washed away. The ice melts, the world changes. But here it is. The proof.

MAU   We were a great Nation.

DAPHNE   You are a great Nation.

ATABA   Imo be praised for making this so.

MAU   We have science, what need do we have for—

ATABA   But who put science inside us, eh? Who made that possible? Daphne – you have brought back my god.

MAU   The knowledge. The civilization we had. We can be great again.

           Music. The Islanders glimpsed briefly in the land of Locaha appear around them. Inspecting the stars. Studying. Debating. Travelling the world. A vision of the Nation as it once was. Daphne picks up a stone globe.

DAPHNE   Look at this. We're standing on a globe. On top of the world is the South Pelagic Ocean and your Nation. It must be. Before the floods. It's upside down.

ATABA   Look. What are these?

DAPHNE   Goodness. You invented false teeth.

MAU   False . . .?

DAPHNE   Yes.

           Daphne holds the false teeth up and manipulates them.

DAPHNE   'I'm catching very little of what you're saying, Ermintrude. Stand up straight. Remember manners and morals at all times.'

MAU   Daphne. Who is Ermintrude?

THREE

Wiltshire. Enter Grandmother followed by the Five Gentleman of the Last Resort. A Servant follows, spraying them.

G'MOTHER   This is incredible – I always thought you were a myth.

ORANGE   Lady Fanshaw. We are as real as you.

PURPLE   The Five Gentleman of the Last Resort are always here.

GREEN   The power behind the throne.

RED   Ready to save Britain in her hour of darkest peril.

G'MOTHER   And is this our hour of darkest—?

GREEN   You must excuse the spraying, Lady Fanshaw.

YELLOW   Imagine if the Five Gentlemen of the Last Resort contracted the Russian influenza.

ORANGE   Then Britain really would be done for.

RED   Our robust health is an utmost priority.

G'MOTHER   This is our hour of darkest peril?

GREEN   Lady Fanshaw: we have to speak to you in strictest confidence.

ORANGE	Can you be trusted totally?
G'MOTHER	The Fanshaws have been the kingdom's most trusted family since Magna Carta. Apart from Uncle Horace, and he thankfully was sent to Australia.
RED	The Russian influenza has taken a terrible toll.
G'MOTHER	Indeed, the servant problem has become acute. Yesterday I fetched my own bathing water.
PURPLE	Not just amongst the servant classes. The whole country has been affected. We've prevented the true numbers appearing in the newspapers.
ORANGE	But we can tell you. Millions have died.
G'MOTHER	Heavens.
YELLOW	What manner of country will we have when spring finally comes?
G'MOTHER	Are you here to tell me that I am going to die?
GREEN	No, Lady Fanshaw. You're uninfected. We've checked that.
RED	The upper orders have been hit very badly.

YELLOW	Even the royal family.
G'MOTHER	Surely not the King?
PURPLE	In the strictest of confidence. The King died yesterday.
G'MOTHER	God save his soul.
ORANGE	We've lost the second in line.
YELLOW	The third in line—
RED	—the fourth, fifth, sixth.
GREEN	And so on and so on and so on. Death has cut a deep path through everyone who might be King.
ORANGE	Your son Arnold Fanshaw is—
G'MOTHER	139th in line to the throne.
YELLOW	—is now our last hope. The crown awaits him.
GREEN	Here.
	Produces the crown from a box.
RED	He is our rightful King.
G'MOTHER	But he's at the other side of the world. Governor of Port Mercia.
ORANGE	There's a boat waiting at the dock. We must find him and crown him. Britain must have someone to lead us through the dark days and back into the light.

G'MOTHER	I am the mother of the King.
PURPLE	You are.
G'MOTHER	Then it is my duty to lead the voyage. Gentlemen, lady – follow me.

FOUR

Enter Daphne and Cahle, with Twinkle.

| DAPHNE | Twinkle: every book that was ever written is wrong. You sailed round the world and discovered the countries and the animals, you saw the planets and— |

Enter Milo, running.

MILO	Daphne. Trousermen are here.
DAPHNE	My father?
MILO	Come quick. Tell us what he says.

Daphne, Milo, Cahle and Twinkle hurry rapidly to the beach. They discover Foxlip, in tattered clothing and in a terrible state, supporting Polegrave. Islanders gather round them, including Mau, Ataba, Pilu, Marisgala and Milton.

| DAPHNE | Mr Polegrave. |

POLEGRAVE   Miss Fanshaw. Help me.

MILTON   Every man for himself.

MAU   Daphne? Is this your father?

DAPHNE   Foxlip and Polegrave. From the *Sweet Judy*.

MILTON   No bloody way. Bad luck. No women. No parrot.

Foxlip comes round.

FOXLIP   We're free men. You won't keep us here. See?

Foxlip draws a gun.

DAPHNE   (*to Islanders*) Take care. He has a gun, he's frightened. It's a bad combination.

POLEGRAVE   Mr Foxlip. Look who it is.

FOXLIP   Miss Fanshaw. So you speak Ooga-Wooga. Now tell them they're going to guard us. Keep us safe from the cannibals.

MAU   Raiders!

POLEGRAVE   They made us slaves.

FOXLIP   We escaped.

POLEGRAVE   (*weakly*) The Chief is . . .

DAPHNE   Yes?

POLEGRAVE   Cox is their King.

MILTON	I'm a dead man. You're a dead man. We're all dead men.
DAPHNE	Oh no.
MAU	Is that bad?
DAPHNE	Very bad. Cox is . . . there's a . . . darkness.
MAU	Then we must prepare for war.
FOXLIP	(*grabbing Daphne*) Now you lot do as we say or we shoot the girl.
MAU	No. She no belong you. She one of us. She of our nation.
FOXLIP	Speakee Englishee, yes?
MAU	I Chief.
FOXLIP	Ha!
MILO	You mustn't hurt her. I want Daphne to be the woman of our Chief. Put down your weapon and fight me like a man.
PILU	Come back – he'll shoot.
MILO	Fight. Fight. Fight.
FOXLIP	Back, savage.
MILO	Fight me!

Milo charges. Polegrave shoots, just missing Milo. Ataba steps forward.

ATABA   Imo watches here. Imo demands
               peace.

MAU   No – old man.

ATABA   What is your race? It is a half-bake
               land. Late to see the stars, late to
               travel the world.

DAPHNE   Ataba – come away.

ATABA   We are the first people. The wise
               ones. Imo smiles on us. See the light
               of Imo shining in me.

POLEGRAVE   What's it saying?

ATABA   Listen to me. Forget your god and
               your anger. Share in Imo's world. Feel
               the light of Imo pouring over you.

FOXLIP   I know what to do with you.

               Raises gun.

DAPHNE   No.

ATABA   I have seen the home of the gods.

FOXLIP   Say goodnight.

ATABA   Nothing can hurt me now.

FOXLIP   Here comes sleep.

               Foxlip fires. Ataba dies instantly.

MILO   Old man.

MILTON   See the Grandfathers – a thousand
                generations – the wisest and bravest
                of men—

MAU   He has killed our Nation's priest. He
                did not see the world with my eyes.
                But still. There was a wisdom in his
                words. I am sorry for the angry
                words I shared with him. I respect
                and love him as if he were my father.
                I will take revenge.

                Mau charges.

DAPHNE   No! Stop, Mau. They'll kill you all.
                Mr Foxlip, Mr Polegrave: we forgive
                you for this death.

POLEGRAVE   Very kind, I'm sure.

DAPHNE   You were frightened. Angry. I
                understand. It's hard to work out
                who's the enemy. You must be tired
                and hungry. I'll take you to a place to
                rest. (*To Islanders.*) I'll take them to
                the women's place. I'm sorry. There
                are many good white men. One day
                I hope you meet them. Follow me.

                Exit Daphne, Polegrave and Foxlip.

TWINKLE   At–a–ba.

CAHLE   Not now, Twinkle.

FIVE

—

A hut. Daphne brings in Foxlip and Polegrave.

DAPHNE   You can sleep in here.

POLEGRAVE   We can take it in turns – in case the
              cannibals attack.

DAPHNE   Would you like some beer before bed?

FOXLIP   Beer? You mean real beer?

              *Daphne gets out the bowls and cuts
              the fruit.*

POLEGRAVE   Suppose this is a trick. Suppose she's
              gonna kill us.

FOXLIP   Little kid like her?

POLEGRAVE   It's a wicked world.

FOXLIP   Miss Fanshaw – will you be drinking
              the beer with us?

DAPHNE   If you like. Well, I must say, this is a
              relief sitting down to drink with two
              proper gentlemen. I feel so ashamed.
              I've gone native. But now you're here,
              I want England.

FOXLIP   Wherever you go, she's always in
              here, in't she?

POLEGRAVE   Our nation.

Daphne spits into the beer.

What's that?

DAPHNE   Native custom. (*Sings.*)

What have you done, son?
What have you done?
Why is your brother so still?

Travel far enough you meet yourself
Travel long enough you'll be home.

Father, forgive me, we had a fight
I hunted, he was my kill.

FOXLIP   Get on and drink the beer.

DAPHNE   Not until I've sung the song. It's the custom.

Travel far enough you'll meet yourself
Travel long enough you'll be home.

Never return, son, never return
Travel and never come home.

FOXLIP   Waste of time.

Foxlip and Polegrave mock Daphne singing 'ooga wooga' as she sings.

DAPHNE   Travel far enough you'll meet yourself
Travel long enough you'll be home.

Father, I wandered, now I am old
Travelled so far I am home.

Travel far enough you'll meet yourself
Travel long enough you'll be home.

Daphne drinks the beer.

POLEGRAVE   How was it?

DAPHNE   Strong.

POLEGRAVE   How do you feel?

DAPHNE   Good.

FOXLIP   Bottoms up!

DAPHNE   Wait. You must spit and sing the song. It's the custom.

FOXLIP   I'm an Englishman.

DAPHNE   Please do it. You really must. Mr Foxlip: I'm telling you. Spit into that beer.

FOXLIP   Ha!

He gulps back the beer.

POLEGRAVE   Is it good?

FOXLIP   Not bad. Tastes of nuts and maybe – Uh!

POLEGRAVE   What?

FOXLIP   I . . . can't see you.

POLEGRAVE   What you done?

FOXLIP   Hello? Can't hear you. Emptiness.

POLEGRAVE   What's happening?

FOXLIP   Can't feel you. Only burn.

POLEGRAVE   Help him.

FOXLIP   Smell death. It's – agh – agh – agh!

POLEGRAVE   Help him.

DAPHNE   He poisoned himself.

POLEGRAVE   Bitch.

DAPHNE   I told you. Do the spit. Sing the song.
I gave you every chance.

FOXLIP   You there, Polegrave?

POLEGRAVE   I'm here.

FOXLIP   Kill me, Polegrave. It's so bad. Agh!

DAPHNE   Your arrogance.

FOXLIP   Shoot me in the head.

DAPHNE   It's fascinating scientifically. Every
custom has a reason. And I think –
the spit starts a chemical reaction.
And the song's just long enough to
make the change. So you get beer and
not poison. But you—

FOXLIP   Shoot me!

Pause. Foxlip dies.

POLEGRAVE   You killed him. He was the best
friend I ever had.

DAPHNE	He killed Ataba.
POLEGRAVE	Turn the other cheek.
DAPHNE	An eye for an eye.
POLEGRAVE	Thou shalt not kill. Look at him. Touch him. That's it. Dead body. That's your doing. What does that make you feel? There's a man wants to know where you are.
DAPHNE	Father?
POLEGRAVE	Father? Cox.

Exit Polegrave.

DAPHNE	I'm a murderer. There must be justice. A trial.

SIX

Daphne is standing with the Nation around her.

MAU	A tri-al? What's that?
DAPHNE	A trial is . . . somebody's done something wrong. Like me.
CAHLE	He deserved to die.
TWINKLE	Mama.
DAPHNE	This is what a trial is for. So we can agree – as a Nation – if I've done right or if I've done wrong.

MARISGALA   You want a trial of fire?

DAPHNE   No. We settle it with words. Was what
             I did wrong? Should I be punished?

MILO   No!

DAPHNE   Or were my actions justified? Can we
             agree a precedent for what is good
             behaviour?

MAU   Alright. Let's have a trial. Sit down.

             The Nation gather in a circle.

CAHLE   Daphne was right. She revenged
             Ataba. She is a great woman.
             Everyone say yes.

             The majority raise their hands.

MAJORITY   Yes!

MAU   That was easy. Trial over.

DAPHNE   No. It takes longer. Murder is a
             serious thing. Even if he killed first.
             Even if I warned him about the beer.
             Somebody must accuse me.

MAU   How?

DAPHNE   Describe all the things I did. Say why
             they were wrong. Why I should be
             punished.

MAU   I see. Anyone?

Silence.

MAU   You better do it yourself, Daphne.

DAPHNE   But I can't be my own . . . Alright.
             (*To Marisgala.*) Here – you be me.

             Marisgala steps forward.

DAPHNE   Men and women of the Nation – if
             each of us seeks revenge then we
             create a culture of barbarism. This
             woman witnessed a murder and so
             she responded in turn with an act of
             murder. For the sake of progress and
             for the sake of humanity I implore
             you: find Daphne guilty!

             Nearly everyone gets to their feet.

NATION   Guilty!

MARISGALA   No!

MAU   Daphne, you're guilty. Can we stop
             this now?

MARISGALA   Will you stone me or burn me or exile
             me or—?

DAPHNE   No! You haven't heard the case for
             the defence. Someone must say the
             other point of view: that I did the
             right thing.

CAHLE   I will do that. Killing is no answer to
             killing. That is true. But it wasn't

	Daphne that killed him but his own arrogance. He killed himself.
MAU	Let's have a vote. Guilty? Not Guilty?

They vote. Exactly half and half.

MAU	It's the same. What do we do now?
MILO	Mau, you are Chief: you decide.
MAU	Daphne – the real Daphne – stand there. Daphne, I . . .
DAPHNE	Mau. Before you decide. You should know. When I first met you, the very first time on the beach, there were words in my head. The same words that Foxlip and Polegrave used.
MILTON	He's a rather marvellous specimen, isn't he? One day I'd like to make a presentation about him to the Royal Society.
DAPHNE	What an interesting specimen of a savage.
MILTON	White thing. Ghost girl.
MAU	Each of us has learnt.
DAPHNE	When you came towards me I was scared and I . . . what did I do?
MAU	I don't remember.
DAPHNE	Yes, you do. You do. Tell them.

MILTON   I've warned you and now I'm going
          to – Bang!

          The Nation are outraged.

MAU   But you didn't hurt me.

MILTON   I've got a fire-maker, thank you.

DAPHNE   I would have killed you if I could. I'm
          no better than Foxlip. The only
          difference is he had a gun that worked.
          How do you find me? Guilty? Not
          guilty?

MAU   Daphne . . . this is difficult . . . it's so
          hard. Everything is grey.

DAPHNE   But you must decide.

MAU   Daphne you are—

          The beating of drums off.

MAU   (*looking through telescope*) The
          Raiders are coming. Prepare for battle.

          *A great commotion as everyone
          prepares.*

DAPHNE   Were you going to find me guilty?

MAU   There's no time for this.

DAPHNE   I don't blame you.

MAU   The trial is over.

> *He levels the gun at Daphne but then points it in the air and fires.*
>
> We are at war.
>
> *An Islander runs in.*

MAU No man's life matters now. All that matters is the honour of the Nation. Into battle.

SEVEN

The beach. The Raiders come on to the beach, drumming and chanting.

RAIDER Locaha: bring death here. Locaha: bring us flesh. Locaha: let us live for ever.

Several more Raiders enter with a massive effigy of Locaha, around which the Raiders dance.

RAIDER (*as Locaha*) I am Locaha. I bring death here. I am Locaha. I promise you flesh. I am Locaha. Worship me well and you will live for ever.

Enter Cox, fully dressed as Raider Chief.

COX   Slaves and flesh. The day is ours.
                   Where is the girl? Find her, Polegrave.

                   *Raiders howl with delight. Enter Mau
                   and the Islanders. They have prepared
                   themselves for battle with war paint
                   and weapons. Daphne and a few
                   others follow.*

COX   What are you? Bring me the white
                   girl.

MAU   I am Mau. Chief of the Nation.

COX   Led by a boy? Oh Locaha, is this a
                   trick?

MAU   There'll be no feasting here. No white
                   girl. We will fight you off.

COX   The boy is the joker of the tribe.

                   The Raiders laugh.

COX   See how Locaha watches over us. See
                   how he calls on you to die.

MAU   I warn you. I am a demon. Caught
                   between boy and man. See my blue
                   crab.

                   He holds it out.

                   The Raiders cower away.

                   Your Locaha is not real. That thing
                   there is a puppet, a toy—

The Raiders howl.

That is nothing like the Locaha I know. And here: because I have seen Locaha, I have been to the land of the dead and I have lived, see I have – a silver dream fish.

Mau holds up the fish, which glints in the sun.

RAIDER He has seen Locaha. We cannot fight him.

COX Stay, you fools. Look how small he is. Can't you smell his fear? Bring me the girl and I'll spare the rest.

MAU No.

COX Let the killing begin.

Milton flies in.

MILTON We're all going to be took just like my boy was took. Let it take yer.

COX It's the parrot. Still not gone? I'll get you now.

Cox fires. Milton falls. Daphne rushes forward.

DAPHNE Milton.

MILTON To justify the ways of God to . . .

Milton is silent and still.

DAPHNE	Oh Milton. No.
COX	Miss Fanshaw? So changed. You've let the sun burn your flesh.
DAPHNE	You too, Cox. We're alike.
COX	(*touching his Raider clothes in a moment of self awareness*) Yes. We are.
DAPHNE	What do you remember, Cox? Wiltshire? The house, the hill, my birthday? The globe you gave me? Benjamin, my friend, your boy?
COX	I have no boy.
DAPHNE	Why did the influenza take him and not me? Why is death so blind?
COX	Nothing.

Cox charges towards Daphne. Mau grabs her away.

I must have her! Into battle!

MAU	Wait. There is another way. If two Chiefs decide, then their armies need not fight. Then the two Chiefs fight in single combat. Whoever wins gains power over all the other has.
COX	That's your challenge?
MAU	It is.

MILO   No, Mau. We'll all fight.

MAU   I've decided.

MILO   You've been a good Chief. You've been brave. You've made wise decisions. But still – you are a boy. In a fight—

COX   I accept. And if I win – the girl is mine. Her life and death.

MAU   You'll never win. Everyone. Leave the beach. This is a fight between two men.

DAPHNE   Mau. His gun. He has six bullets and then he has to reload.

MAU   Six bullets.

MILO   Come little bird. Rest now.

Milo picks up the still Milton. Everyone leaves the beach until just Cox and Mau remain.

COX   I do remember a boy. Another world. Another life. And he's telling me: kill you like all the rest.

The world slows down. Many Maus appear.

MAU 2   See how it all slows down.

MAU 3   See how clear it all becomes.

MAU 4   How bright the sound.

MAU 5	Think how sharp your senses must be.
MAU 4	And how fast your mind is racing.
MAU 3	How can you win this fight?
MAU	Are you all of you me?
ALL	Yes.
MAU	How many are there?
MAU 2	More than you can ever count.
MAU 3	Each thought you think.
MAU 4	Each choice you make.
MAU 5	Makes another Mau.
MAU 2	Maus.
MAU 3	That could be.
MAU 4	That will be.
MAU 2	You are never alone.
MAU 3	Look into your enemy's soul, Mau.
MAU	It's too dark.
MAU 3	But you must look inside him if you are to beat him.

Mau looks at Cox. Cox moves in a slow, ritual, almost dance-like way. Mau imitates his gestures and echoes his words.

COX/MAU   There ain't nothing above. I look up for lights and signs. A hand to show me. Nothing there. Nothing below. I search down for justice, for punishment, but there's none. I look forward – no meaning there. Back – and there's emptiness. And all I live in now is anger and hate. Every breath I breathe is destroy. And I will destroy you, Mau.

MAU   Where should I go? What should I do?

MAU 5   The sea.

MAU 4   That is your world.

MAU   Yes.

MAU 3   Run.

Mau reaches out, throws sand in Cox's eyes and runs.

COX   Agh! I'll get you, boy! There's no escape!

Cox pulls out his gun, fires.

Mau is swimming under the water.

MAU 5   You're safe in the water.

MAU 2   But when you come up to breathe—

MAU 3   Ah yes, when you come up.

MAU 4   What then?

MAU	(*struggling for breath*) Oh.
	Mau surfaces for a moment to gulp down air. Cox fires.
COX	I'll get you.
	Mau goes under the water.
MAU 4	Quick. What did you see?
MAU 3	Six barrels.
MAU 5	Six bullets. Two gone.
MAU 2	Four bullets left.
MAU 3	Swim further, harder, but still you're going to have to—
	Mau surfaces for air. Cox shoots again.
COX	Closer. The next one is for you.
	Mau is under the water again.
MAU 2	Three bullets left.
MAU 4	Hard now.
MAU 3	Fear and exhaustion.
MAU 2	But you must win.
MAU 5	For the Nation.
MAU 3	For Daphne.
	Cox is in a canoe now. He paddles out into the lagoon and then lets it drift.

COX	One night Locaha spoke to me. Not their painted god. But the real thing. And he said to me: 'To die is easy. Why are they so afraid? What do they want? To live for ever? Far worse.' And I said: 'You're right, Locaha. Just not for me. My boy. Don't bring death here.' And he said: 'That's what everyone thinks. If only *I* could be spared. You're just the same as everyone alive.' And that's the night I said: 'There's only one power worth having in this world and that's the power to kill.' Come on, you bugger. Up and breathe. Cox is going to kill you good this time. Come on!

Mau comes up to breathe. Cox fires. He hits Mau's ear.

A hit. Are you dead?

MAU 5	Two bullets left.
MAU 2	Blood.
MAU 3	Your ear.
MAU 4	Blown away.
MAU 5	Don't stop.
MAU 3	See blackness.
MAU 2	Use the pain.

MAU 5	Sharpen mind.
COX	Blood? That's good. Because you know what blood means don't you? Blood means . . .

Sharks appear in the water, circling Mau.

COX	They're hungry. Who'll get you first?
MAU 3	Not much time.
MAU 2	Before the attack.
MAU 4	If he uses the bullets.
MAU 5	He must reload.
MAU 4	Give you time.
MAU 3	Make him use.
MAU 5	The last bullets.

Mau bobs up.

MAU	Cox!

Cox fires.

COX	Games, is it? Dead man's fever?

Mau bobs up in another place.

MAU	Cox!

Cox fires.

MAU 3	Six bullets gone.
MAU 5	Now he's reloading.
MAU 4	Now is the time. Now.

A piece of driftwood floats above Mau.

MAU 3	It's there.
MAU 2	The tree from the boy island.
MAU 4	Remember what you did as every man has done?
MAU 5	Remember how you . . .

A brief vision:

Mau raises an axe.

MAU	Mah!

Mau brings the axe down hard until it is stuck in a tree.

An explosion of birds in all directions calling out in warning and alarm.

MAU 4	Waiting for you there.
MAU 3	Just where you put it so many moons ago.
MAU 5	A silver string from there to here.
MAU 2	There is your weapon. Quick. On your own.

The other Maus go. Mau pulls himself up on to the drifting tree. Cox is reloading the gun.

MAU   Cox.

Mau pulls at the axe in the tree.

COX   What's that? Ain't got the strength?

Mau struggles.

You're never going to do it boy.

Mau pulls the axe from the tree and from there leaps into Cox's canoe.

What's this? You ain't gonna – please. I got no bullets in this. You play fair, don't you? Put down your weapon.

Mau puts down his axe. Cox pulls out a pistol.

I got this. Because I don't play fair see? I—

MAU   No!

Mau throws himself at Cox. The gun goes off in the air. Cox falls on the edge of the boat.

COX   Don't let me fall in there. They'll eat me.

MAU   Goodbye. Bad meat.

Mau pushes Cox over the edge of the boat.

The sharks come together and tear Cox apart, feasting on him.

No more blue crab.

Mau rips off the blue crab and throws it into the sea.

Enter Milton, flying but rather unsteady.

MAU   Milton! You survived!

MILTON   I don't play fair see? Knickers. A little fruitcake.

Milton flies off. Mau slumps back, exhausted.

Locaha appears to Mau.

LOCAHA   That was a great victory. You're not a boy now. Or a man. You're a hero. You've done everything you can in this world. Time to let it go. Time to move to another world.

MAU   What do you want, Locaha?

Everything is empty apart from Mau and Locaha and white light.

LOCAHA   This is your world.

The Nation gradually begin to appear.
Some are farming, some are looking
after children, some are making beer,
a trial is being held.

LOCAHA It is a hard place. Year after year, the
Nation's crops will fail. People will
starve. Brothers will fight. Love will
end in disappointment. Mothers will
see their babies grow sick and die.
Sons will grieve the death of fathers
over and over for ever more.

MAU I know.

LOCAHA But you don't have to go back there.
A very few men – whose deeds are
greatest of all – go to a better world.
Here is the door. Let me open it and
you can step straight in.

Locaha opens the door and we see a
glimpse of an Eden.

LOCAHA Step in and leave this imperfect world
behind.

Mau moves to go through the door
but finally turns back.

MAU No. I will go back. The imperfect
world.

LOCAHA If that is your choice.

Closes the door.

You will never see Paradise now.

MAU   Will I see you again?

LOCAHA   Every man must face Locaha. But not
               for a long time now. You will live to
               be older than you can ever imagine.

MAU   And Daphne?

LOCAHA   I can't tell you that.

MAU   You must.

LOCAHA   Mysteries, worries, sufferings. The
               world you've chosen.

Locaha disappears.

EIGHT

*Suddenly Mau is back on the island. A young Islander,
i-To, runs up to him.*

I-TO   The water in the stream is cloudy,
               Chief.

MAU   That's because there's a pig stuck
               upstream. Take a stick and push the
               pig out of the water and then the
               water will run clear.

I-TO   Yes, Chief.

*i-To runs off. Enter Daphne with
Twinkle, now two.*

DAPHNE   Look at this, Mau.

TWINKLE   'Travel far enough you'll meet yourself
Travel long enough you'll be home.'

DAPHNE   He's only just two.

Pause.

What are you thinking about?

MAU   Last year. The time I killed Cox.

TWINKLE   Twinkle twinkle little star
How I wonder what you are
Up above the world so high
Like a diamond in the sky.

MAU   I was thinking . . . There are so many
worlds. There's a world where there
was no big wave.

DAPHNE   A world where all your people are
alive.

MAU   That world exists. Yes.

DAPHNE   And if you could go back and be in
that world, is that where you'd want
to be?

MAU   No.

DAPHNE   Why?

MAU	Because in that world I would never have met you.
DAPHNE	Oh.
MAU	Somewhere there's a world where there was no Russian influenza, no *Sweet Judy*, no Captain Roberts, no Milton. Somewhere where your mother and your brother didn't die. Would you choose that world?
TWINKLE	When the traveller in the dark Thanks you for your tiny spark Then you show your little light Twinkle twinkle all the night.
MAU	What would you choose?
	Enter i-To, running.
I-TO	Quick – there's a boat.

NINE

Daphne's Father enters. He is followed by several Soldiers. Enter Milo.

FATHER	Good afternoon. Are you chief here? I come as a friend. I know you don't have much English but . . .
	Marisgala and various Islanders enter. The Soldiers raise their guns.

FATHER   Put them down. No guns. Hello. Can
any of you understand me? Please
help. I had a daughter once. They
told me that she was surely drowned
during the big wave two years ago.
But I won't believe that. I've been
travelling from island to island. There
are so many hundreds of them. But
I must find my child.

MILO   You sound serious. But about what?

MARISGALA   He's speaking trouserman. Daphne
would understand.

*Daphne enters with Mau, Pilu, Cahle
and Twinkle.*

FATHER   My daughter had the most wonderful
advantages. She knew about science.
Observation and experiment which
allow us unfold the mysteries of the
planet. All of this is yours – if only
you'll help me find—

DAPHNE   'I should say from the number of
steps taken – five thousand and forty
two – and the scent of beech and the
merest hint of cowslip that this is
Duffer's Hill. Am I right? My
deductions are usually right.'

FATHER   What was that?

SOLDIER   Your Excellency?

FATHER	I heard my daughter's voice. Who spoke?
SOLDIER	Just a savage, Your Excellency.
FATHER	But it was English. I could have sworn—
DAPHNE	'Oh, my word. With these lenses I calculate I should be able to see . . . Saturn first, I think. Thank goodness the night is so clear. I'll look now and take notes later.'
FATHER	Those are my daughter's words – as she spoke them. Who said that?
DAPHNE	I did.
FATHER	How do you know those words?
DAPHNE	Daddy. Have I changed so much?
FATHER	Can it really be you? Ermintrude?
DAPHNE	No. Not Ermintrude. I'm Daphne now. But I am your daughter.
FATHER	Oh my dear girl.
	Father falls to his knees. Daphne runs to him and they embrace.
DAPHNE	Mau – come and meet my father.
MAU	Daphne taught me how to do the hand-wiggle thing. (*Shakes his hand.*)

DAPHNE	Mau is Chief. Daddy – this is our Nation.
MAU	Make welcome to Daphne's father.

The Nation begin a welcome ceremony: loud and cheerful.

Enter Grandmother with the Five Gentlemen.

G'MOTHER	Stop this! Stop this now!

Gradually the ceremony tails away.

FATHER	Mother.
G'MOTHER	Arnold, there have been a great many deaths caused by the Russian influenza. Particularly – I must report – amongst those of royal blood. All of them dropping away until finally . . .

Grandmother curtsies very deep.

G'MOTHER	Your Majesty.
FATHER	Good God.
DAPHNE	Daddy! You're King of England!

Daphne ululates.

G'MOTHER	Who is that little native girl making so much noise?
DAPHNE	It's me, Grandmother.
G'MOTHER	Oh God.

Grandmother nearly faints and
collapses to her knees.

ORANGE There there, Lady Fanshaw. It really
has been a very long voyage.

PURPLE Now, Your Majesty, I'm afraid we
have to move fast. We have to get the
crown on your head as quickly as we
can.

FATHER But Westminster Abbey is continents
away.

YELLOW And of course, we'll do all that in
time. But for the moment . . .

PURPLE We're going to perform a temporary
coronation. Is there a congregation?

DAPHNE Yes.

The coronation is prepared for. The
Five Gentlemen supervise the rolling
out of a red carpet.

ORANGE Anything to sit on?

Islanders appear. One of them brings
a stool, which is placed at the head
of the red carpet where a throne
should be.

The Islanders form themselves along
the red carpet.

FATHER Is this actually happening?

*Grandmother puts an ermined cape
on Father's shoulders. Father proceeds
down the carpet. Father sits. Mr Red
proceeds down the carpet with the
crown and then raises it high above
Father's head. Mr Green and Mr
Yellow place the sceptre and orb in
his hands.*

RED   By the power invested in me by
               Almighty God, I crown you King of
               the British Isles and Emperor of all
               her sovereign dominions. God save
               the King.

ALL   God save the King.

FATHER   Mother, Daphne.

G'MOTHER   Daphne?

FATHER   I would like to say a few words on
               this historic – and quite extraordinary
               – day. Some years ago I lost my wife
               and child. And I couldn't find it in my
               heart to forgive a god who could take
               them away. So I came to the other
               side of the world. And then – darker
               still – I thought I'd lost my last
               precious child to a great wave. I
               almost gave up on living altogether.
               But today to find myself so happily—

YELLOW	I'm so sorry, Sire. We have to set sail straight away. You have a country and an Empire to run.

Mr Green removes the crown.

GREEN	We'll look after this on the voyage home.

As quickly as it was set up, the coronation is dismantled. The cape is taken from Father's shoulders.

Mr Red takes out a Union Jack on a spike.

RED	I claim this island for the great British Empire, the biggest Empire the world has ever—
DAPHNE	No.
MAU	We don't want to be part of Empire.
RED	But we can offer you great learning, trade, government—
DAPHNE/MAU	No.

The Soldiers raise their guns.

FATHER	Do as the Chief says. Take the flag away.

The Soldiers hesitate, look to Mr Red.

It is my order – as your King.

RED	Sire.

Mr Red takes the Union Jack away.

MAU	Thank you, Sire. Sire: I want our Nation be member of Royal Society that Daphne has told so much about.
G'MOTHER	Ridiculous!
FATHER	Yes. I command that your entire Nation become affiliate members of the Royal Society.
MAU	Our island be place for scientists. They will come here and study all we learnt thousands years ago.
FATHER	This is a place of learning?
DAPHNE	There's so much to see here, Daddy. It's incredible.
MAU	And when scientist come, they must bring us tool, instrument, medicine. The nation must progress. And every scientist come he must give a – what's word? Daphne? A— (*Mimes.*)
DAPHNE	Lecture?
MAU	Yes, lecture, so that we know all the thing that happen in science. We are hungry for new knowledge.
FATHER	I will make sure of it. I will come back myself if there are things to be learnt here.

DAPHNE	Oh Daddy – you won't believe how much. We can turn the world upside down.
FATHER	(*laughs*) I'll need proof of that.
DAPHNE	Not a problem, whatsoever.
RED	All ready to go now. All on board.

Exit the Five Gentlemen, Grandmother. The Nation start to move away.

DAPHNE	Daddy, I want to stay here.
FATHER	But I've searched for you. Many years.
DAPHNE	I can't leave Mau. I have to—
FATHER	Please, no. All of this (*King's robes*) is nothing if . . .
DAPHNE	I want to be with you in England. You'll be the best King there's ever been. But. I want to be here, the Nation. I want . . .
FATHER	Dear God: Don't take her away now.
MAU	Daphne? You're a princess. You have duties. Wiggle my hand. Goodbye.
DAPHNE	Mau, don't—

Father stands alone as Daphne talks to Mau.

Which world would I choose? I choose this one.

MAU   One day you will be Queen of the trousermen. That is your world. You must go to it. There is something more important than me and you. Nation.

Enter Grandmother, carrying a large formal hat.

G'MOTHER   Ermintrude – I think you've caught quite enough of the sun already. Put this on, dear.

Daphne turns away from Mau and walks over to Grandmother, who puts the hat on her.

There we are. Now if you'll only stand a little straighter. You're first in line to the throne.

FATHER   Mother. There is no more Ermintrude. This is Daphne.

G'MOTHER   Daphne? I'll do my best. Yes. It suits you. Daphne.

FATHER   Come on Daphne. Let's go home.

Enter Milton.

MILTON   There's nothing that a cup of tea can't put right, don't you find?

DAPHNE   Milton – are you coming with us?

MILTON	Off we go. Come hell and high water.
DAPHNE	That means yes.

Father, Grandmother and Daphne go to leave.

DAPHNE	Just one word.
FATHER	Of course

Exit Father and Grandmother. Milton stays and watches.

MAU	Daphne. There are no words in anyone's language to say this.
DAPHNE	Yes.

Daphne and Mau stand and look at each other for a very long time. Then Daphne mimes 'sad'. Mau shakes his head and mimes 'happy'. Daphne mimes 'happy'.

Enter an Old Man with two Children, all in modern clothes. They set up a telescope.

MAN	Who wants to look at the stars first?
GIRL	Is this the place where Mau and Daphne said goodbye?
MAN	So they say. But it was a hundred and fifty years ago, so who can really be sure?

BOY	And scientists have been coming to this island ever since?
MAN	Oh yes. Charles Darwin. Albert Einstein. Richard Dawkins. Darwin was particularly fascinated by our Grandfather Birds.
GIRL	Did Mau and Daphne ever see each other again?
MAN	I don't think they did, no.
BOY	Oh.
MAN	Well, she was Queen. Got married to a Prince from Holland. But on her deathbed the history books say she asked to be brought back to this island. So in 1928 her body was flown here. Mau had died only days before. And both their bodies were given the traditional ceremony and sent out to sea side by side.
BOY	Where they turned into dolphins and swam together for ever.
MAN	I'm not sure about that. That sounds a bit like a story to me.
BOY	I think they became dolphins.
GIRL	And so do I.
MAN	Well, it has a sort of sense. Even if it's not very scientific.

BOY	And is it true you can still see Mau's ghost standing watching after Daphne every night?
MAN	That really does sound like a story.
GIRL	Sir, does Imo exist?
MAN	Does Imo exist? Well . . . humans exist. And so we'll keep on asking: 'Does Imo exist?' for ever and ever.
BOY	Are you crying?
MAN	I am a bit, yes.
BOY	Why?
MAN	Because. Because you're young and full of questions and that's the best thing in the world. Come on. Let's look at the stars.

They look through the telescope during:

MILTON	Goodbye, Mau. Goodbye, Daphne.

They kiss. Exit Daphne. Mau stands alone for a moment. Enter Cahle.

CAHLE	Twinkle is asking questions. Who made him? Why did Ataba die? Does Imo exist?
MAU	. . .
CAHLE	Are you watching her sail away?

MAU   I'm looking after the Nation.

*Cahle exits. Mau watches out to sea.
Two dolphins play and sing as Mau
looks out to sea and the Old Man
and the Children look up at the stars.*

End of play.